Water Treading in Serious Earth

Poems By: Michael Francis Wright

World Peace Revisited

World Peace!
Like the Tiniest Molecule of a Molecule
      Of light that started our Big Bang Boom
      Explosion from love:
      Sprung from Inner Peace!
I had A Vision of World Peace!
      A picture of when we were the first
      Amino Acids creating the first living
      Cells Eternally Evolving back to the spiritual
Totality.
Everybody let down their borders!
      Walls crumbled, border lines evaporated,
      Mental blocks and shields Collapsed;
      Awakening Awesome trust
      For the Universal
      I AM!
We the people of Earth!
      Our new pledge of allegiance to
      Ourselves to everyone, who is
      Everything including us.
Everyone was Loving!
      Ourselves, you, me, trees, leaves, stones,
      Animals insects all brothers and sisters
      From the same One
      All the same stuff; All distinct
      All in love; All were love!
Everybody Buddha, Christ, Krishna, Lao Tzu,
Yahweh, Allah.
      Troubadours of Spirit!
      Angle Song writers of the same Phrase!

Everybody Peaceful!
   Not necessarily quiet; But At Peace
   In yin yang balance
   Oneness surrounding our spiritual selves
   Alpha waved good by to Past Prejudiced
preaching
   A Crystal Lake of Light Lifted Bodies!
The United States of Earth!
   Our new national nemesis
   Echo playing our new found Awakening
   Eternal Oneness
   Inner Peace
Nobody fighting!
   Ended Wars, fights, Arguments, conflicts,
tussles
   Clear minded, non-selfish, what's mine is
yours
   Attitudes over powered he evil of the
frightened past
   Lives once frittered away by
       Possessions, Oppressions,
Disillusions, Confusions
       Simplified and Simplified
       No Borders, No wants, No fears in the
simplified mind
Everyone giving!
   Tithing to everyone
   Who was acting without doing, and working
without effort
   Enhanced Mind body, Sister Brother
Connection

World Peace!
>Everything was happy in this dream vision
>A quantum leap to
>>Inner-Outward, Self-Not-Self, Spirit-
Non-Spirit,
>>Sameness Peace
>The moon didn't need to be in the seventh
house
>>And Jupiter had no need o align with
Mars
>>And still peace guided our planet
>>And love enthralled our homes.
World Peace!
>Mahayana, Catholic, Hinayana, Protestant,
Jew, Muslim, Hindu
>>Same things, Same people,
>>Same teachings, Same spirits
>All the same
World Peace!
>Led to by Inner Peace that Unlocked
>And unlatched the bolted doors
>Battered Down By Inspired Enlightenment
Yeah;
World Peace.

Evaporating Illusions

You can't kill anything
That is Alive
Cause all that lives
Will never die
Life is the force
Life is the love
Life is God
Everything is God

Walking on this Earth
I ask my self
When did world get swallowed by illusion?
When did world forget they made it themselves?
Cause society spreading illusory ways
Instead of journey within
They wanna journey without
Mind thinks out
But soul sits within
Where everything is known

Abundance of oneness
Can be witnessed all around
Your eyes peal different
Cause you think your restricted
Your restricted cause you mind's control
        can't be your goal
Cause freedom of your mind comes
        in it's submission to soul
Seek journey within and judge no sin
Weak people will scare you with burning

But everyone knows we are all learning
Every minute of the day
Every witnessed event
Every unseen knowledge
Kashic records can be tapped
Just allow your soul to remember
The all of everything.

WHOLESALE CHANGE
All around us nature cries

While politicians pass out
Propaganda pamphlets preaching
Ignorance to the signs
Insects are dying
Animals are dying
Earth Moans for repair
What keeps politicians
From acknowledging despair
Alarm bells have been tolling
For a hundred years
Still oil companies drill
Pumping ancient sunlight
Sucked from soil
Instead of absorbing new
Out of thin air
Radiation therapy clinics
Million dollar health benefits
Doctors proctor growth cancerous
Insane asylum is fill with
Tree huggers who demand more oxygen
Soul of solar system knows it's tiny
Man thinks he owns what he sees
Mad Earth groans for us to stop
"Sop up your tears", they say
To dreary environmentalists
"We're not burning it's just warm today"
College students pass by
On their way to classes
To learn to think for themselves
50% will learn & know

While 150% left will go
To the chambers of greed
Pay only mind to riches
Feeding fire of economic flames
Disasters loom in sunset haze
Smog infested cities
Cause, well, "You don't expect us to <u>really</u>
change?!?"
Democracy is in the hands of 500
While billions are screaming to be
Heard in a cloud that surrounds
TV marketers won't change
Unless best interest bottom line is made
Unfortunately best interest is investment
And pennies pinched for greed mongerers
But everyone wants money
More so than clean air to breath
Suffocation smolders in heated reproduction
Perfectly happy with lungs muddled
Perfectly happy with cancers caused by over
destroyed nature
The wild is known as troublesome
Unwilling conformers unconscious
Continue to be misinformed
The answer is ,
Change Everything.

HEART CONDITION

Everyday another news announcement
Scandal in government
Embezzlement in businesses
Blood in Urban & Suburban streets
Country roads to smuggle victims
Heartbreak everyday all day long
Preparation for forming storm
Running blindly into abyss
Looking forward formulations
They want global control
They want us to lack self control

So they can sell us complete control
So they can tell us it's for our own good

See fear filled shit - Hear fear filled shit
Smell fear filled shit - Taste fear filled shit

Accepting fear in forgetting love
Heart condition - Conditioned Hearts
Not hard to see why we – so willing
Reactions in fear breed fear
Reflexes in fear bring fear
Humans gotta hear - we gotta drop fear
We're not going anywhere
We're making it harder
Harder to stay earthbound
Hardened hearts - purple hearts
Subliminal systems teach
Competition instead of Cooperation

Create better soil for growing war
Global war is what they want
Hearts must stay strong- keep the beat
Keep on beating - stop your bleating
You are sheep no more
Follow inside to guide life -love- living
Breath within in meditation
To defend your heart against despair
Defend against corruption of self
Keep heart strong in love momentum being
Look government–business–Institution in eye
Say clearly with strong voice
There's a new way coming today
Conditioning hearts to love
Stop making loving hearts fear

Heart conditions made for making love
Heart conditioned for connection
Heart conditions changing already
Just thought alone is amazing
Amassing a shift in consciousness
Helping us drift away from fear
Protocol no longer lingers in command
Self control - cooperation - contemplation
Drop need idea to bring wealth without cash
I'm getting carried away
It's just a matter of heart condition...........

Human Shift

Rebooting Consciousness
We are the great shift
In momentum toward
Inevitable Critical Mass
Process of roping in new
With calm commentary
Describing reality a new way
We are Cause & Effect
Cosmic process impressed
We are shift happening

Stone age – Bronze age
Iron age – Industrial age
Modern age – New age
Old age – Space age
Unnamed age – Conscious age

Comprehension of intention
To grow understanding
To know individual
One with cosmos
Relative world
Where we are all relatives
Connected Oneness
Impressed divinity power

Gotta know your power
Gotta know you are power
Use your power

Inflect
Reflect
Detect

Change is constant
Let it guide us conscious

Life As War

Coliseum is ruins
Windows burned out
Fumed gunneries frighten memory
Corrosion of dreams
Gladiators – gone – generation
Time flows with spinning stars
Shooting across stagnate sky
Manmade mountains pyramid mingles sky
Desolation marches – in uniform
Nuclear evaporated beings
Skeleton x-ray invisible skin
Life as War
Soaring passed light years of human movie
Mathematics – binary – digits – Alpha Omega
Einstein
Electric grid maps plot power and defense
Crashing waves – storm sea green information
Eclipse sun with modulation domino-effects
Searing mental-scape – marching armies
Mind control tactics instilling fear in pure sense
Faceless masses maiming faceless bomb builders
Maiming humanity as if ants were marched on
Missiles – pistols – air – land – sea Attacks
Relativity theory creating big bang destructible
Earth
Meteorological maps making mayhem in oceans
Keyboards line fields – hands type
In infamy in cosmic kaleidoscope fractals
Paisley worm holes launching new skies
Slow salt ocean begins to rumble

New Storms foamy salt bubbles swimming soldiers
Beakers full of next agent orange nightmare
Chalk white skeleton gaining flesh
Eyes on sperm squirming uteruses
 Like million human crowds below microscopic
Machine-man living bodies turning spinning
Vertebral column brain waves babies
Created to destroy babies all around them
Light forms Dolly genetic life formed by science
Gymnastics march country – vs. – country
Imaginary enemy of games of human brains
Fierce force of muscles making ideas of stronger
Running naked man hammers out pure hot steel
Marathons waves – sine – cosine – tangent ribbon
ballet
Swards swing flip skylights in out human muscle
Pumping fast heart – hard competition jumps higher
Dancing legs ice skaters discuss throwers
Pole-vault sprinting steroids rushing perfection
Generations and generations repeating each other
Gentle touch of hand who became hardened
Soul of human endeavors in gestures
Motives smiling actors laughing
Directing soft elegant movements
Smiling human faces loving each other
Conversations in slow motion capture
Inner dialogue gleans wheat fields
Humor each other in oneness loveliness
Crops uniform in rushing harvest
Deforestation – Dams – hydroelectric
Highways harnessed with automotives
Checkered flag sky view skyline motherboard

Rushing vehicles passing below like bits
In gas cloud oil field
City programmed computers developing black hole
Tornado cones gentle flowing smoke
Evaporating lines lights ellipse
Flags float in breeze – united nationalism
Money makers waving in unison crowd
Confetti marchers horns – lock parade
Political marches Hitler in stock market
Corporals in business fighting business
Crowds in stadium casinos vie for
Camera space pushing – points of view
Perpetual peace negotiators
Boxer goes down for counting cards
Red carpets bear world's wet dreams
Fame fortune spectacle waving hello world
Ranting fans shimmering glow highlights
Rockets to outer space laser dome
Boy scouts ready for battle
Money power greed machine stock traders
Launching fireworks reminding war
Screaming fans waving spirals down
Smoke begets itself in mist illusion....

Locked in a Curve

Pale face
Eyes blue
I might be swimming in you too

Face blue
Eyes pale
Swimming in my mind without fail

Eternity waits
Mortality skips
Then and now here the entire trip

Waiting aghast
Beauty grasped
But only the mind is exercised time's elapsed

Curl in hair
Curves up and back
Ignite the heart beat tingle the body press back

Living with Venus
Penetrate no moon
Hot blooded sun Gemini proof.

Love's Asleep Dreaming With Me

I love you like yesterday and before and after
You've gone to sleep
Just as I'd promised
I'm on bunji chord temporarily dizzy
I've just leaped for sum total heart heave
The sun is staring me in
Faces of serenity I am with you
In your dreams – In my dreams
I am doing flips hiding what's
Inside the vehicle you tell me
The tales of getting tail and
You've gone to sleep
I want to taste the glow
On your cheeks
I want to ponder the scent
Of your lip balm on my lips
I want to carry passion from your eyes
I am looking in your eyes I am dreaming
You've gone to sleep and now I see peace.
You've gone to sleep
My love's sleeping
My love's bursting at seamlessness
I'm quiet with my deep love
I'm silent but in my dreams
I speak flowing lyrics of your
Ear begging passion I am blossoming lotuses
In my dreams with you I'm magic
I make birds sing I free them from cages
I love birds my bird
My feather Skimmed Angel Moon child
My night passenger – you're next to me

I want to taste your light again
Like we did way back when the dew
On our heads new in sparkling sun rising
To greet our poet eyes
I want to dance in the ocean of your intention
You've gone to sleep
I am sleeping too
I am waiting till we both can't help ourselves
Again.......
I am waiting for you to come again
You are constant glow inside my heart
I know you will never leave me
You know our oneness now first hand
The world knows when a poet's heart goes out
When a poet's heart goes out it never stops
It is constant everywhere
I am here with you
On my way to add to these lines
When I was pinning about what to write
I saw your glory rainbow across sky
There was no rain today except in my heart
But I knew you were with me then too
I know you can never be far for love never departs
My love I saw you just the other day
We shared our last smoke our last vocal lines on
the phone
Hours later there were no more except your
whispers
Don't worry Michael
I'm sorry Michael I am here Michael I Love You
Michael
Whispers inside my telepathic soul mind

Our transcendental love drive
This new hurricane this new history you've created
with us all
I am your first prophet I know you are Buddha
And plotting your bodhisattva return
My sojourner my perfect consort
My glowing guide light steering me clear
You are the moons child and mother of us all
You decided it was time to get off the phantasm
merry-go-round
Here we are to see you've gone to sleep to
remember again
Now you remember again eternality of your soul
Whispers and music I hear in my spinning heart
Whirlwinds of memories fill my core you're soothing
me now
Hesitation holds me in golden brightness of your
face
Your glimmer burns my eyes with pleasure
I see your great ascension right around the corner
galactic seconds away
Glance next at the newness of your babe self soon
Our dawn will end and new age will begin Aquarian
dream vision
The next rotation of our sun around our universal
soul
That one verse that fills us all universal whole
I am oneness in you – bright faced in our
remembrance
She knows you care because she feels your truth
Knows your honesty feels your sincerity
Climactic visions I tried to peal from my brain

Formatted to these expressions
My love is sleeping
My love is everywhere is everything dreaming
awake
Like ocean waves shifting sands of the undertow of
timelessness
Consecrating imaginations in all creators
cooperating
My love this world is not ready our crawling legs
must walk
In these last breaths of this cycle
This world is not ready, but slow progress
becoming steady
For your tsunami of loveliness we scurry to make
preparations
Our hearts and minds slow to dance in passion
Wipe clear the windshield of our inner eyes and
ears
My love you are sleeping and I am with you
My love you are sleeping and You are with all
My love you're sleeping
You know the frequency of ripples you are creating
this moment now
You know limitlessness of undying soul
My love never leaves my love is eternal like all
My love is sleeping awake in our hearts and minds
My hypothalamus is pondering what concoction to
create
To link us two for so long I am waving hello to say
goodbye

I heard your cries and now the apple is gone from my eye
I had not the answers to diminish demons
My soul understands my mind crams for the right expression
My body is shaking shaken crazy trying to keep my feet
Hearing me today and seeing me yesterday you know
My love you know
My love hello love hello
How a decade grows and exposes the beat soul
Your true beat soul your beatitude wholeness
I am with you my love you are sleeping awake
My love I could write forever, but these people must go home
I love you my Love hello!
Namastē my beautiful entities
Namastē my friend my love my Joy
Namastē my Joy
Namastē
Joy

Mountain Walk

Here high
On mountain
Leaves fall
Only muffles
Motors below
Hum Hungry
No desire
On mountain
Me lone
Human soul
Walking Crest
On old
Mountain path
Rocks history
Modern man
Dew drop
In cosmos
Work pray
Every day
With tomorrow
Better than
Now calliope
Factory Labor
Wearing ties
For disguise
Needs proof
Illusion looters
Corrosion continuers
I breath
Fresh Air

Between smog
Same air
And exhaust
Fume scare
Beg silence
Poison Illusion
Drifter confused
Pen ink
Paper pad
Using last
Drop reality
In all
Secret waits
When dualist
Demise reveals
Relative oneness
With All
Already In
Rabbit hole
Turn Yourself
Into wizards
Diving All
Nature creates
Own power lines
Climbing surrounding
Man made vines
Captured time
Gripping illusion
On mountain crest
Radiation shrills

In my brain
Is it the sun?
or just my mountain?
Chopper cops
Above heat
Dharma Echo still
I standing collect fall's
Leaves falling in my
hood
Amen
A man
One man
Women
Whole man
Amen
All men
Omen
Oh man
Om Mani
Om Mani
One many
Omen Amen
Aman A man
One man kind
Amen A men
A many man Om

No Children Play In The Park Today

Warm late summer
Sunshine all day
Clear skies Pennsylvania
Empty ballpark
Deserted swing sets
Slides only for spiders webs
The children of America are inside learning to die
Killing each other on video web based games
War games to corrode childhoods
War games to desensitize smiling faces
War games to train a new generation of fight
squads
Line up oh teenager! Line up!
Get in line to join America's war machine
Grinding our 100% American human beef
To dye front lines red without restraint
To die front lines careless army – ants to squash
Just graduated – got G.E.D.
Training only takes a week
Then say hello to Iraq, Iran, Afghanistan!
Bombing out citizens for or against Bush games
Playing Doom, Resident Evil city streets towns
Erupting in bar fights mindless violence
How can it be? Who goes looking for a fight?
Have you seen?
Have you seen TV and movie screens
Screaming with global disaster.

Path of Dark Jungle Life Light Formulations

Building a lifetime
Thoughts, memories, and moments
Conjuring current conception
Corrections come constant
As illusion whips one off feet
Swift descent brings contemplation
Hmmmmm how has his happened – Not
Happenstance
Modulating movements make
Momentary defeat into reason for success
Decisions made – make new streams
Appearing in cracks of monuments of belief
Growth comes lucid light bright shinning
Spotlight pointing concepts splintered together
Gathering similarities snowball rolling trajectory
speeds
Warping understanding into new perspective image
inspection
Postulating probability binary turns possibility in
stereo
Becoming polyphonic rhythms of it's own virility
Creation one cell – one person – on communion –
one world
Microcosmic mirrors macrocosm man pondering
Wandering and never lost
Even when seams burst
And all seems lost
All one is never alone
Ghost knows where to go.

Pee Wee-Island: Gone Now

We arrived at our childhood
Stopped with eyes zombied
Mouths dangled wide open
            Nothing could have prepared us
            For the clusters
            of houses
That infested our wilderness
            playhouse.
Treetop forts
Tangles of bush and vine overgrowth
Run through and climbed
In childhood ghost hunts
We had our own Sherwood
To hide from a frightening adult world
It was our utopia
A childhood commune ruled by
            unspoken laws
It was the one string of freedom in
            conformities noose
The woods at PeeWee Island
Now a virtual wasteland of suburban
sprawl
We cried that day
hysterical
For all our nature
Destroyed to greed
Going
Going
Gone…

Prison Prism

Prison prism - Put myself in - Locked inside
Shamed location boxed - postage paid - sealed for delivery
I search the corners - The cracks in light
The doorway is wide open - My legs won't walk - Body won't budge
Stuck in fear-Fading slow- Into Love
but the box is years tall -- The prison is decades thick
the locks not broken - But with all my might - I pry at the bolts
they'll loosen as soon as - the door is ajar - And my light explodes - Bolder before my cave quarters
Nickels and dimes don't save a penny – Dollar bills destroy my dreams
While attempting to put me back together -- I fall apart at the seamless
Suicide of my elders and fortress builders
Buy your life away ---- toys toys and more toys --- waist time with toys
ignore all signs of Goddess speaking to society of suckers
Perpetuation of tense living conditions
Livin' the good life slave to money
no freedom in that --- no freedom in here
Did I mention that I'm in the USA --- ---
Land freely taken from others -- Won't prosper in the end

Just goes to show you - your bliss and comfort tear
you down
When you rule with fear in fear to fear for the good
of fear
All you get is disaster after disaster
Failed system after failed system built on another
Let the sent be the heard -- Let the sent be the
word
Know the message is the same in all names
No One will go without after fears gone
I just have to follow the lead of my own pen.
Ascending to freedom I am air floating past cell
bars
I walk through the box in and out and the air is
clearer out side here.

Rainbow End Eyeshine

We found rainbows' end
staring awestruck at it's glows
Got out car dancing

You stayed in car where
You smiled at watching me walk
Through glowing spectrum

My body feeling
Layers energetic glow
Vibrating higher

Before the day low
Feeling stress from illusions'
Imprinting mind hope

Cleaning slate clean
No effort needed in pain
Release illusion

Know perfection works
Through portals unseen but known
shine with eye's smile

Rapids In The Soul Stream

I was on the bridge
Of transcendence
Just when I think I know
Just where I think I want
Finally having secrets revealed

CRASH - - SMASH - - BLANK - - BRIGHT
Fights with fear only acknowledge it
Only way is train it away Blank Fear Out

I finally know something
I think I feel perfect
Where I am cause my master plan's
A mystery and only know by union
Between conscious and subconscious
Bless The Moment of Great Horned Calamity
For these are moments of great change
And you must trust the ghost's great plan
Sometimes hidden from conscious thought
Can be Totally Creative Thought
Is Manifesting Desire at the Speed of Belief
Speak Peace – Know Peace – Feel Peace – Share
Peace – Grow Peace
If it is peace your desire wants to vibe into
Of course true course is your own personal course
The sway of solitary psychic – meta – physic Soul
Stream…

Sea New To Be Now

The looking glass ponders
Possibility creeks in flow
Flooding bank of brain cells
Celebrating mutations powerful
Perspective gives golden observation
Oblivion is lost to truth
Turning key unlocks seal
Suppression of ability
Unwrapping stagnation's ramparts
Redefining relation to material
Mayhem hindrance trashed
Tributaries of capability fracture
Foundations of creed's traditions limiting
Leaping forth with mediation
Meditation conjuring new parameters
Punctuated with infinity symbols
Symbiotic understanding of energy
Emotive force of mind eye
Elementary electrical understanding
Undermine obtuse education imposed
Inspiration from Intuition's connection
Conception of new humanity
Harmonious All to self to else to other
Old ways fade like paint in sun rays
Ramifications breed fortifications
Freedom's most emancipated moment
Movement from ideas of weakness
Wilting to blossom ideal to power
Propagation brought into ambition
Answers from examples shared scene
Simple eternity experiential

Sea New To Be Now

The Answer...(talking to myself again)

When You find the answer
     And the answer is inside You
There's no other choice
     But to go–in to find out who
To find out Your selfless self
To interact as highest self
That is to say one self
That is to say one aspect
That is to say spectral analysis
Of personal mutation of divine
Of personal formulation of god-ness
Nestle Yourself within Yourself
Submerge Yourself within Yourself
Marinate within Your soul
Then You will know
There will You find it
Then You will see
There will You figure it
Then You will listen
There will You hear it
Now You Will BE It
And it starts by selecting what brings You down
Examine every aspect of Your now
As a citizen of slave state
Examine how they control Your happiness
Explore other options
See addictions inside & out
Let them fall – and see clear without
Need controls – Greed controls – Fear controls

See them all & let them fall–drop them now
They don't serve You – They serve to keep You
down
Do You feel Yourself? Clean it out– now wash it
new
Now it's time for You to do what You do for You
See suffering & feel suffering & hear suffering
Now unlock cages – kick doors out – open windows
Let air in – breath deep – feed fire of creation
Light streaming from lucid body
Illusion seen past looked beyond
AWAKE
You must make it happen
If You want it to begin
There is no other choice
Except - Accepting What's Within!!!

Accept what's within
Not what's outside- Trying to tell You to doubt
Not what's outside- Trying to tell You what it's about
Not what's outside- Trying to tell You to pout
Not what's outside- Trying to tell You to buy & sell

Turn off TV – Turn off everything –
        Begin paying attention to breathing
        Soon – as You relax – You feel heart beating
        Feel total self – feel layers
Feel energy clouds surrounding suffusing
Infuse – Light within – Go within – Go within –
Be Your source
Induce Your whole to know every level of soul

Practice Practice Practice& Soon See Ease day to day
Embodiment is a decision on multitude of levels
Accept what's within
Unlock what's within
Inspect what's within
Reflect what's within
Detect what's within

You keep asking when
I'll say the same thing every minute
Go within or go without
You want answers as to how
Go within or go without
You wanna know the way out of suffering
Go within or go without
You wish to make yourself into something
Go within or go without
The Answers are waiting for You quietly
While You settle down – While You open Your ears
While You are ready to hear, with nothing to fear
The Answer Will Be Found .

THE HEAVY LOAD OF FRIDAY

Heavy load of Friday early
Work begun it's 5am and
I have nothing to do
But still my head full
For strain of seeing straight
Four days of work
One right on top another
Each day realize dreams – In mind
Each day finalize plans – In thought
Each day surmise goals – In dream
Each day get home and
Finally realize too tired
Too tired to create dreams
Each day, I could Each day, I may
Each day, I want Each day, I mean
Frustrating when you swim
In sea of possibilities
Procrastination mimics in mental control plots
Possible moments movements reflex dissects
My soul patient – my brain anxious –
My mind antsy
I am at ease, and still linger hungry angry
Unfolding and closing – circling, Unfurling
Processes clogging momentum
purposeless slave life accepted
'gotta pay rent'
purposeless slave life expected
'gotta eat right?'
purposeless slave life inherent
'gotta pay bills'
Purposeless consumption planet

Perpetuate broken system empire slave state
Just to live life in the bankers' wet dream
I'm called a crazy dreamer
Just for thinking to improve life for all
Templates taking control technological
Harness power of automation total
Personal progress to render & mold
Awaken inner conductor
Prowess to remake Earth sustainable
Reading till late night
Self imposed study
Researching means to change
Society that's deranged
Raging in monopolized markets
Heaving heavy loaded self control
In couch potato factory - warehouse - jail house
Revamping brain cells to amplify protocol
Originate away from vampire status quo
Rebooting hard drive to include cruise control
To be true rebel don't let society swallow you
As you create new ways to improve
And the heavy load of Friday is removed
While ripples reverberate and make us new

Then Truth Becomes Authority

Traffic constant crashing waves
Everyone's hearing it in silent times
River rolling quiet under tone
No birds heard cold wind passing winter noon
Passed tree limbs bending tilting soundless
Distress is impressed by casual acceptance
Revolutions reserve rights on ramifications
Fortifications seem only to help enemies
Who have we garnered against us?
Who can separated what's only one?
Will a mass proceed to caress ideas of oneness?
I and You are really one entity Earth
Really one with universes seen and not
Sadness sucks the sting out of separation
Emancipation fills feeling full of oneness
Sweet success is only-truth's success
Help doesn't hinge on the owners, users, seducers
Medusa lives inside the TV sets sitting before
thoughtless
Masses meander motionless accepting all the box
brings
Murdered dreamscapes detoured goals
To service self destruction – personal mutilation
See through tangled lie web – slip passed rocks of
conformity
We'll only pull through when truth becomes
authority.